Godot, Alive or Dead

Books by Nathaniel Hutner

Heracleitus Under Water   1988

War: A Book Of Poems   2003

The Name We Never Lose   2019

The Complete Poems of Nathaniel Hutner   2021

Plays by Nathaniel Hutner

Godot Arrives

Godot Imagine Godot

Godot at Night

Godot, Alive or Dead

The President Pardons Godot

Short Plays by Nathaniel Hutner

Hot Potatoes

The Fix

Keewaydin Plays

Godot, Alive or Dead

೫ഠ

A Drama by Nathaniel Hutner

Burlington, Vermont

A collected edition of Nathaniel Hutner's plays, *The Collected Plays of Nathaniel Hutner*, is available from Onion River Press, 191 Bank Street, Burlington, VT 05401

Copyright © 2021 by Nathaniel Hutner

All rights reserved. No part of this publication may be reproduced, distributed, or transmitted in any form or by any means, including photocopying, recording, or other electronic or mechanical methods, without the prior written permission of the publisher, except in the case of brief quotations embodied in critical reviews and certain other noncommercial uses permitted by copyright law.

Onion River Press
191 Bank Street
Burlington, VT 05401

ISBN: 978-1-949066-91-3

Library of Congress Control Number: 2021913982

Designed by Jenny Lyons, Middlebury VT

Godot, Alive or Dead

CAST OF CHARACTERS

GODOT

LADY DALY: a large black woman in her early thirties, manic-depressive with aggressive tendencies

DOTTIE DUMPLING: A maid, thin

UNCLE STURTEVANT: A Southerner suffering from megalomania

DANIEL: Black-haired twenty-two-year-old, very handsome

ALICE: Waitress (former Princess)

LUCILLE: A Society Person

MR. MALAPROP: A loose tongue

LANCELOT BROWN: Former Resident-in-Chief of Westchester Clinic, attached to Lady Daly

POPE

CARDINAL

CANDY/SHEPHERD

PERDITA/SHEPHERD (Candy's sister)

ACT I

SCENE 1

First, a mental hospital in Westchester County, as in Godot Imagine Godot. Afterwards, a barren waste in the Outer Hebrides, as in Godot Arrives.

> GODOT
> I think I've used up everything, including myself.
>
> LADY DALY
> Nonsense. You're depressed.
>
> GODOT
> But we are free.
>
> LADY DALY
> That's why we are all depressed.
>
> GODOT
> I guess life is not such a great gift, after all.
>
> LADY DALY
> It depends whose life you are talking about.
>
> DOTTIE DUMPLING
> I like to clean.
>
> GODOT
> That's my job. I'm the responsible party.

UNCLE STURTEVANT
We are all the responsible party.

DOTTIE DUMPLING
Look at me!

(They all look)

DANIEL
Even I am responsible, and I'm still an adolescent.

GODOT
You're precocious.

DANIEL
So are you.

GODOT

(Laughs)
Every time I drop trou, someone notices.

DANIEL
We are only trying to help.

LADY DALY
Yes.

ALICE
We do love you.

GODOT
Love, love.

ALICE
Is it such a bad thing?

GODOT
It seems to excuse a lot of things.

DOTTIE
We love you without excuse.

DANIEL
Mr. Godot, Dottie and the rest of us are quite sincere.

GODOT
What of all the rest we have left behind?

LADY DALY
They have earned their fate.

ALICE
And we have earned ours.

LUCILLE
And what is that?

GODOT
Perpetual happiness? I am only guessing.
(Pause)
Think about it.
(They think)

GODOT
Is that really what you want? Eternity? Happiness?
(They all think some more)

UNCLE STURTEVANT
Well, at least we are not crazy any more.

DOTTIE
You can appreciate my labors.

GODOT
You can all appreciate your own.

ALICE
The sunset is nice.

DANIEL
Girls are sometimes beautiful.

GODOT
You can be beautiful.

LADY DALY
We can all be beautiful.

LUCILLE
That is true.

GODOT
But the rest?

DANIEL
The living?

GODOT
Yes.

DANIEL
They are falling into eternity, and they have no idea where it will take them.

LADY DALY
Where?

GODOT
I can no longer see into the future.

DANIEL
That is because you are dead, too. You have assumed your mortality. And here is where you end up.

DOTTIE
But where are we?

LUCILLE
With each other.

DOTTIE
But where?

GODOT
At am asylum, some 30 minutes by a short drive north of New York City.

LUCILLE
Something is becoming clear.
(They all look at LUCILLE)

LUCILLE
Life had its purpose. Death does, too. Like life, it has the purpose we give to it.

DOTTIE
You see!

GODOT
What about happiness? What about eternity?

UNCLE STURTEVANT
Straw dogs. Just like me. I used to think I was everything. Now I know I am nothing.

DANIEL
And the rest of us.
(To GODOT)
You have made your choices. You are still free to make more. We are all free to make more.
(Light begins to dim)

LADY DALY
The sun is setting.

GODOT
It is time to act.
(They all look at GODOT)

DANIEL
Action is dear.

LADY DALY
Words are not.

DOTTIE
Are we moving?

GODOT
You will see.
(Slow fade to BLACKOUT)

ACT I

SCENE 2

        DANIEL
There is no way out of here.

        GODOT
We are all free to leave.

        DANIEL
What about the living?

        DOTTIE
We can haunt them.

        LUCILLE
We already do.

        LADY DALY
Where are they?

        DANIEL
Outside.

        LADY DALY
Outside what?

        DANIEL
Outside us.

UNCLE STURTEVANT
This is getting us nowhere.

MR. MALAPROP
This is where we are.

GODOT
One puzzle after another.

ALICE
Maybe we should stop thinking.

LADY DALY
Maybe we should do something.
(Pause)

DOTTIE
Time is passing.
(She dusts)

GODOT
I suppose I should help clean.

UNCLE STURTEVANT
Haven't we been here before?

DANIEL
Where?

UNCLE STURTEVANT
Immobilized.

GODOT
What?

UNCLE STURTEVANT
By anguish.

DANIEL
Godot was in anguish. Don't you remember how he writhed on the floor?

(All nod)

DANIEL
(Continuing)
He set us free.

GODOT
You have always been free.

DOTTIE
I need to move, constantly.

LUCILLE
I enjoy watching the weather.

UNCLE STURTEVANT
It seems to move.

LUCILLE
What can move us?

ALICE
A little genealogy.

UNCLE STURTEVANT
Presumption.

DANIEL
Sex.

LUCILLE
Alcohol.

LADY DALY
Food.

DOTTIE
The four food groups.

LADY DALY
Alcohol, caffeine, fat, and sugar. I love them all.

GODOT
(Pauses)
Which way are we going now?

DOTTIE
The dust is not very heavy today.

GODOT
You needn't collect it, my dear.

DOTTIE
Well…

DANIEL
Is there love in youth?

GODOT
I never had a youth.

LUCILLE
And old age?

GODOT
Do I look old?

LADY DALY
Does anyone here look old, now that we are dead?

DANIEL
We are subjects of arrested development.

UNCLE STURTEVANT
I was once arrested, for threatening suicide.

DANIEL
Really?

UNCLE STURTEVANT
They locked me up in a hospital, not like this one. For three days. As a precaution. And they gave me pills. They made me sleep. When I woke up…

DANIEL
Back to suicide?

UNCLE STURTEVANT
That is the story of my life.

LUCILLE
And mine. Alcohol is a slow way to go.

DOTTIE
If you dust, you die only at a great age. My grandmother was 95 when she went, and she had dusted for ages.

GODOT
The common lot.

DANIEL
Where do I fit in? I don't dust, and I have never contemplated killing myself.

UNCLE STURTEVANT
You will.

LUCILLE
Then you will be an adult. Welcome to the club.

DANIEL
I don't think I want to grow up – at least not any further.

GODOT
You won't.

LADY DALY
You are already dead at an early age. Now the only thing to do is make peace with yourself.

DANIEL
You are very philosophical.

LADY DALY
Kid, with my experience, either you learn or you die.

LUCILLE
Or both.

UNCLE STURTEVANT
I think we are doing all just fine.

DOTTIE
We are keeping each other company.

ALICE
The conversation is interesting.

GODOT
There are no authorities.

LUCILLE
I feel a little faded.

MR. MALAPROP
Comme ci, comme ça. Or, as it were.

GODOT
I must stretch my legs.

LADY DALY
I must stretch my mind.
(LADY DALY looks at the audience)

DOTTIE
I must stretch the dust, or I shall have nothing to do for eternity.

LUCILLE
I must stretch my drink.

UNCLE STURTEVANT
I am going to stretch my power.

DANIEL
And I, my love.

GODOT
I shall stretch time, all of it.

DANIEL
I am learning about string theory.

GODOT
That will help.

ALICE
I want to stretch myself.
(There is perfect silence)

MR. MALAPROP
The truth seems to be elastic, strings or no strings.

UNCLE STURTEVANT
I can pull strings.

LADY DALY
Is that why you are here?
(There is silence)

LUCILLE
I experience oblivion every night.

LADY DALY
Lady, you sure do get your exercise.

ALICE
I am afraid of my inferiors.

DOTTIE
I will put salt in your coffee.

DANIEL
I need technical sex training.

GODOT
At your service.

DANIEL
You! Again! I thought we broke up in the interregnum.

GODOT
That was just a rest period between bouts of intellectual and emotional creativity.

LADY DALY
I'll create you, if you don't watch out.

GODOT
I think I shall go back to being alone.

UNCLE STURTEVANT
So that's where you come from!

DANIEL
Now we know.

GODOT
You do not know where I come from. You cannot guess what preceded my solitude.

(They are all stumped)

DOTTIE
A little rag?

GODOT
Practically.

LADY DALY
Nothing!

GODOT
Now we revert to what we know.

LADY DALY
And we cannot know nothing because nothing does not exist!

GODOT
Lady Daly, you are the crown jewel of humankind. I love you.

DANIEL
We all love you.
(GODOT looks slighted)
DANIEL
(To GODOT)
I think you may be an imposter.

LANCELOT BROWN
Here I am!

LADY DALY
I thought you had rejoined the living.

BROWN
We were divorced, but I still love you.

LADY DALY
Ready for Round Two?

BROWN
Now that we are no longer married, we can enjoy ourselves.

LADY DALY
Promiscuous!

BROWN
Psychotherapists of all conditions prescribe love as the best cure-all.

GODOT
What is love?

ALICE
Where are we going?

LUCILLE
It's alright, dear. I was really only interested in your real estate.

MR. MALAPROP
I resign.

DOTTIE
From what?

MR. MALAPROP
My position as Sibyl.

LADY DALY
How many positions did she have?

MR. MALAPROP
It is easier to be a stenographer.

GODOT
I can see we are re-casting ourselves in a new light.

ALICE
What?

LUCILLE
What?

GODOT
Even though we are dead, we are subject to change.

DOTTIE
I want to be myself, permanently.

LADY DALY
I don't ever want to be myself again.

MR. MALAPROP
Slower, please, I am trying to take notes.

GODOT
Don't. They won't be of any use; where are we going, the uses of history are extinct.

DANIEL
But we are extinct.

GODOT
That is what I have been saying all along.

MR. MALAPROP
Where is A? He has missed the whole show!

LUCILLE
A no-show.

DANIEL
I'll show him.

MR. MALAPROP
What?

DANIEL
What, what?

MR. MALAPROP
(Patiently)
What will you show him?

DANIEL
We can all change.

ALICE
Especially in his absence.

DANIEL
Godot has been absent for a long time.

UNCLE STURTEVANT
And now that he is here?

DANIEL
He is still a no-show.

GODOT
Which is why you are all free.

LADY DALY
Thank God!

GODOT
Thank me.

ACT I

SCENE 3

        DANIEL
I just want to write.

        GODOT
Write what?

        DANIEL
An autobiography.

        GODOT
But you're only twenty.

        DANIEL
Twenty-two.

        GODOT
Even better.

        DANIEL
Two years can make all the difference.

        GODOT
Do I make a difference?

        DANIEL
Yes.
(GODOT and DANIEL kiss)

DANIEL
Now, you'll never go back to women.

GODOT
You are handsome.

DANIEL
Really?

GODOT
I am known for my good taste.
(They kiss)

DANIEL
Delicious.

GODOT
How far do you want to go?

DANIEL
Just a kiss. For now.

GODOT
You tantalize me.

DANIEL
I am still a virgin.

GODOT
I am not.

DANIEL
Ah, well.

GODOT
Do you love me?

DANIEL
Sometimes.

GODOT
You continue to tantalize me.

DANIEL
I want you to build up some steam.

GODOT
Something is building up.
(GODOT puts his hands between his legs)

DANIEL
Here. Some grated potato, egg, milk, onion, and a frying pan with some oil.

GODOT
Where's the oil?

DANIEL
Here.

GODOT
Oh.

DANIEL
There is nothing like one of Aunt Gertrude's potato pancakes with applesauce.

GODOT
I like French.

DANIEL
French what?

GODOT
Food.

DANIEL
This is more substantial.

GODOT
Good God!

DANIEL
These are just the preliminaries.

GODOT
I hope so. Are you sure you don't want to go out? French cuisine is the highest of them all, except, perhaps, for the Chinese.

DANIEL
They will eat anything.

GODOT
So will I.

DANIEL
Behave!

GODOT
I am trying.

DANIEL
It isn't every day that I prepare dinner.

GODOT
It isn't every day that I offer myself to someone.

DANIEL
It can wait. You yourself said we have eternity in front of us.

GODOT
We do.

(GODOT looks auguished)

DANIEL
In that case, we have time for potato pancakes.

GODOT
I rather like French food.

DANIEL
I am sorry. Anyway, you are repeating yourself.

GODOT
I'll try not to. But with so much time to pass…

DANIEL
Things could get a little dreary. Even love.

GODOT
Yes.

DANIEL
Has this happened to you before?

GODOT
You have no idea.

DANIEL
I can imagine.

GODOT
Life is too short.

DANIEL
Death is beginning to look too long.

GODOT
That is why I clean out the memory every so often. Then I can repeat myself without knowing it.

DANIEL
What?

GODOT
If I have to face eternity, I'd like to do it with you.

DANIEL
The pancakes are almost done.

GODOT
So am I.
(GODOT puts a hand on DANIEL'S thigh)

DANIEL
Oh….
(BLACKOUT)

ACT II

SCENE 1

Enter all the actors from Act I dressed in black academic gowns, except for GODOT, who is dressed in white priest's vestments and DANIEL, in combat fatigues.
Stage Right – a throne. Throne is occupied by the POPE, who is dressed as a clown.

    POPE
Sit down.
(They all sit)
    POPE
(To GODOT)
Who are you?

    GODOT
Don't you know?

    POPE
I ask, you respond. Who are you?

    GODOT
I am Godot.

    POPE
And who is Godot?
(GODOT is silent)

POPE
(Continuing)
Does anyone here know this soul?
(There is silence)

POPE
(Continuing)
Speak up. Does anyone know who this man is?

DOTTIE
He helps me clean.

UNCLE STURTEVANT
He has fixed my brain – and my family relations.

LADY DALY
We're pals from way back.

LANCE
He has brought me down to earth.
(POPE raises eyeglasses)

LANCE
(Continuing)
Well, when we were alive, he brought me down.

POPE
Anyone else?

ALICE
He has given me a job which I enjoy.

POPE
(To ALICE)
You look familiar.

ALICE
Your Honor, we have had several audiences together.

POPE
Yes. You are a Princess.

ALICE
I was a Princess. Now I am a waitress at the Hard Luck Café, here in Heaven.

POPE
Yes. I think you have waited on me.

LADY DALY
We have been waiting on you for a long time.
(The POPE ignores LADY DALY)

DOTTIE
(Hopefully)
We enjoy our work.

LUCILLE
I am a socialite, and I can vouch for Godot. His lineage is spectacular.

POPE
Thank you. Anyone else?

DANIEL
We are lovers.
(The POPE looks interested)

DANIEL
We are monogamous.
(The POPE shrugs)

DANIEL
We have been waiting for Mr. Godot for a very long time, and now he is here.

UNCLE STURTEVANT
He is not what we were expecting.

DOTTIE & OTHERS
No. Not at all.

POPE
What were you expecting?

DOTTIE
Well, something like you. A little flashy, with some music, background lights, massive architecture, and an aquiline nose.

POPE
Nose?

DOTTIE
You do look aquiline to me.

LUCILLE
To me, too. Very distinguished.

POPE
Thank you. But you are not here to flatter me.

LADY DALY
We were wondering, now that we are in Heaven, if you could judge us. Sort of set your seal of approval on us. Make us feel at home.

DOTTIE
And secure.

GODOT
You see –

POPE
Not you.
(To DOTTIE)
Continue.

DOTTIE
We don't want to go back.

LADY DALY
And we need to know who Godot is, or was, or –

POPE
What makes you think this is Heaven?

DOTTIE
There are no trees.

LUCILLE
Or grass.

UNCLE STURTEVANT
Or flowers.

GODOT
Rather like the Outer Hebrides.
(The POPE nods)

GODOT
(Continuing)
O!

DANIEL
There are lots of clouds.

LUCILLE
It is just as I had imagined it.

DOTTIE
Yes. And it is not dirty.
(DOTTIE looks a little despondent)

DOTTIE
(Continuing)
What am I going to do?

POPE
But what makes you think this is Heaven?

LUCILLE
No cocktails, not even any family trees.

LADY DALY
I don't see too many Black people here.

POPE
Most of them are in Heaven.

LADY DALY
If they are in Heaven, where are we?

GODOT
The Outer Hebrides.
(At this point, a SHEPHERD BOY appears, dressed in a kilt)

GODOT
Oh, someone young.

DANIEL
Competition.

POPE
Quiet!
(To the SHEPHERD)
Do you know where you are?

SHEPHERD
I am lost.

POPE
Where do you come from?

SHEPHERD
My village.

POPE
And where is that?

SHEPHERD
In the Outer Hebrides.

GODOT
I told you so.

POPE
Are you looking for something?

SHEPHERD
I have lost my sheep. I fell asleep – I am all alone – sometimes I must sleep – and they wandered off. If my master finds out.

DOTTIE
We can help you look for them.

UNCLE STURTEVANT
Of course.
(The others agree)

GODOT
Can you point us in the right direction?

SHEPHERD
I don't know.
(SHEPHERD begins to cry)

GODOT
It's all right.
(The others begin to see that the SHEPHERD, besides being young, is also very beautiful)

LUCILLE
Well, dearie, would you like me to make you some lemonade?
(SHEPHERD nods no)
(LUCILLE makes some anyway)

LUCILLE
Here. It will take your mind off your troubles.

DOTTIE
Let me clean your shoes.

(DOTTIE takes them off and begins to clean them)

LADY DALY
Do you like music? I was in a Brooklyn choir. Baptist. Very high church.
(SHEPHERD doesn't know what to say)
(LADY DALY sings a hymn)

LANCELOT
I didn't know you could sing.

POPE
Stop!
(LADY DALY stops)

POPE
This is not a circus.
(Everyone begins to laugh – as the POPE is dressed as a clown)

POPE
Stop! Stop!
(They all laugh louder)
(The POPE begins to smile. Then he laughs, too)

GODOT
Make I speak now?
(POPE keeps laughing)

GODOT
It seems we have returned to Earth.
(Everyone stops laughing. POPE exits)

LADY DALY
No joke?

GODOT
No joke.

DOTTIE
Why?

LUCILLE
Anyone can see why. To help the Shepherd, of course.

UNCLE STURTEVANT
What about the Pope?
(Everyone suddenly notices the POPE has disappeared)

DANIEL
Some joke.

ALICE
But where is he?

GODOT
I have sent him back up into The Clouds.

UNCLE STURTEVANT
Uh – oh.

GODOT
Purgatory.

LADY DALY
Were we ever in Heaven?

ALICE
I was once a Princess, and it was not Heaven.

UNCLE STURTEVANT
I was once Emperor of the Universe, and it was Hell.

DOTTIE
There is no garbage in Heaven.

SHEPHERD
(Hopefully)
There is no garbage here.

GODOT
Right.

ALICE
Then this is Heaven?

GODOT
This is the Outer Hebrides. For the time being, you are in Heaven.

LADY DALY
You mean –

GODOT
Yes, Lady Daly. Heaven is a state of mind, not body, and you are all in it.

SHEPHERD
And me?

GODOT
You are a treasure whom all of us respect.

DOTTIE
I loved him at first sight.

GODOT
So did we all.

SHEPHERD
Can I go now?

DOTTIE
But we want you to stay.

SHEPHERD
But my sheep –

ALICE
They are lost.

GODOT
Yes.

SHEPHERD
I must find them.

ALICE
May we help?

GODOT
Of course. That is why we are here.
(Everyone begins to smile a lot. They point to each other's heads as if to say "Heaven")

LANCELOT
This is the price we pay for our sins.

UNCLE STURTEVANT
Sins?

LADY DALY
I know about sinful, and we aren't it.

GODOT
Yes.

LADY DALY
We are sick.

DOTTIE
And now we are well.
(The SHEPHERD leads them all offstage)

ACT II

SCENE 2

         DANIEL
(By himself)
  I wonder where they have all gone…
(He wanders around stage absent-mindedly, then sits on a rock)

         DANIEL
  I could sing.
(He tries a hymn)

         DANIEL
  Ugh.
(He tries a Broadway show tune)

         DANIEL
  Solitude is confinement.
(He gets up and resumes wandering)

         DANIEL
  I hope I don't spend eternity alone, here.
(There is a crack of thunder)

         DANIEL
  I think salvation is near.
(The POPE appears, dressed in Papal vestments)

POPE
Greetings.

DANIEL
Hello.

POPE
Where is everyone?

DANIEL
I think they're resting.

POPE
Good idea.
(The POPE smiles widely. Daniel looks alarmed)

POPE
And you, dearie, how old are you?

DANIEL
Thirty-nine.

POPE
You can't be more than an adolescent.
(DANIEL does not respond)

POPE
You are very handsome.
(Pauses)
Was that your father with you?
(The POPE imitates GODOT in a gesture)

DANIEL
We are just friends.

POPE
You said you were lovers.

DANIEL
It's platonic.

POPE
I am not a follower of Plato. In fact, I have never read him. He is a bit too much of an Idealist. Long-winded, too. I prefer Heracleitus, or, maybe Parmenides.

DANIEL
Or maybe –

POPE
(Cutting him off)
You are a student somewhere?

DANIEL
I have no home, and I only have myself to study.

POPE
What about Godot?

DANIEL
He is only a friend.

POPE
(Thinking he is getting somewhere)
Do you have any other friends?

DANIEL
Just the ones you have seen.

POPE
But they are all old.

DANIEL
You are no youth yourself.

POPE
I am the Pope!

DANIEL
What are you doing here?
(The POPE ignores this)

DANIEL
(Continuing)
If you are here, you must be dead.

POPE
Pooh. If I were dead, I would not be here, with you. I would be in Heaven.

DANIEL
Or somewhere else.

POPE
(Getting a little agitated)
Look here, I'm the Pope and you are very attractive. Wouldn't you like to get to know me better?

DANIEL
I think I'd rather not know you at all.
(The POPE attempts an embrace)

DANIEL
Get out of here!

POPE
So young and so untender.

DANIEL
I'm leaving.
(DANIEL stays. GODOT enters)

GODOT
Very heroic.

POPE
What?

GODOT
I say your love making is very heroic, but it won't do. It just won't wash at all.

POPE
Wash what?

GODOT
Your soul?

POPE
I am an expert on souls, and you are no one.

GODOT
Yes. Well, I don't see much point in your making passes at young men. You are old, and you have never in your life been very attractive.

POPE
I am the Pope, and I can have what I want.

GODOT
I am Godot, and I think you are making a bad mistake.

POPE
(Indicating DANIEL)
I think it is up to the young man to decided between us.

DANIEL
(To the POPE)
You're just a clown.

GODOT
(Smiling)
In fact, you are dead, and your soul, and a few others, need to be retro-fitted.

POPE
I am quite aware of my soul. And I am not dead. And if anyone here needs a soul, it is you.
(To DANIEL)
And you, too. You should take pity on an old man who has everyone's best interests at heart all the time, except for his own. I didn't want to be Pope. I was chosen – or elected. When

I was a Cardinal, I could do what I wanted. Now, I have to put up with nonsense all the time. It is not fair. I'm supposed to pray half the day, and spend the rest of the time looking after a lot of people just as sinful as I am. I want freedom. But I am Pope and I have nothing, nothing for myself at all.

DANIEL
You have us, if you like.

POPE
How, how can you say that? You both have just rejected me. And you say I am dead. If I am dead, how can I be here with you?
(Alarmed)
Where are we anyway?

GODOT
In the Outer Hebrides.

POPE
I have never heard of them.

DANIEL
I'll draw you a map.
(DANIEL draws on the ground)

DANIEL
(Continuing)
Rome is here, all of Italy here, France next, then the Channel and England, and then Scotland and the Outer Hebrides.

POPE
I am afraid.

GODOT
You needn't be. You are Pope.

POPE
But I have just exposed myself completely.

GODOT
Yes, and it doesn't matter.

POPE
You mean I can do whatever I want?

GODOT
I don't think that is the conclusion I would draw. But, yes, you are free to do what you want.

DANIEL
What do you choose to do?

GODOT
(After a pause)
We are here, waiting.

DANIEL
Here we are.

POPE
O, can't you just leave me alone? O, that is your line.
(DANIEL laughs. GODOT looks pleased)

POPE
O, I am even more afraid of you now. How can I do the right thing? O, I am so compromised!

GODOT
Not at all. You are dead. And you can do whatever you like. Just like life.

POPE
But I told you when I was Pope, but I still am Pope, or perhaps – am I really dead?

GODOT
I see a big "D" on your forehead.

DANIEL
Today is Ash Wednesday.

POPE
And I am dead.
(Big pause)
Well, I guess running after Daniel isn't my prime object in life – in death.

DANIEL
You will find many more like me if you stick around.

POPE
I am sticking.

GODOT
I suggest you take a tour of the premises for a while, and then come back and tell us what you think. You may change your state of mind.

DANIEL
That is what I did.

GODOT
Yes. Then you can approach us both from the right point of view. Love need not be ugly.

(GODOT and DANIEL exit together. POPE falls to the ground and begins to cry and tries to pray, but he can not pray)

ACT II

SCENE 3

      GODOT
I was just trying to remind him of what he already knows.

      LUCILLE
That is what we all already know.

      ALICE
I think we forgot it.

      UNCLE STURTEVANT
Somewhere.

      ALICE
Maybe in childhood.

      DANIEL
Or later.

      GODOT
Maybe. Maybe some people never forget.

      DANIEL
And some people never remember.
(POPE enters)

      POPE
O, my brain. I am in such pain!

LUCILLE

I guess if Heaven is in the head, so is Purgatory.

(GODOT smiles)

ALICE

You know, Mr. Godot, we all love you.

GODOT

I believe it.

LUCILLE

Your blessings were definitely not what we were expecting.

UNCLE STURTEVANT

(Somewhat dubious)
Is there more to come?

(GODOT smiles but says nothing)

GODOT

There is always more to come, otherwise you would not be dead. Life is very limited.

(SHEPHERD enters)

DANIEL

What are you doing here?

SHEPHERD

I found one sheep.

(He pulls on a chain he had been carrying that extends off stage. A CARDINAL enters. Everyone is transfixed)

GODOT

Where have you been looking?

LUCILLE

Rome?

ALICE

Boston?

GODOT
Anywhere else?

DANIEL
Take your pick.

DOTTIE
Do I have a clean-up job ahead of me, or what?

GODOT
I must go buy a blackboard.
(GODOT exits)

DANIEL
Uh oh.

ALICE
Now we get a lecture, and I always hated my lessons.

LUCILLE
I had a few lessons.

UNCLE STURTEVANT
And now we are here.

LADY DALY
You said it.

SHEPHERD
Now, I am here.

DANIEL
You must be dead.

SHEPHERD
Me? Dead? I don't believe it.

CARDINAL
(Moaning)
Someone has caught me.

DANIEL
What?

CARDINAL
Someone caught me *in flagrante delicto.*

LUCILLE
With this Shepherd?

CARDINAL
Yes.

ALICE
How did you die?

CARDINAL
The starving masses strung us up.

SHEPHERD
(Offering)
In plain sight of the sky.

CARDINAL
I am guilty of so much.

LUCILLE
Have you ever been out of your mind?

CARDINAL
No.

ALICE
Now that you are dead –

CARDINAL
I do feel somewhat odd. Very peculiar.

DANIEL
He's out of it.

UNCLE STURTEVANT
Let him suffer for a while.

LUCILLE
We'll bring you along in good time.

CARDINAL
Time, time, I had a good time, until now.

LUCILLE
Do you know where you are?
(CARDINAL shakes his head)

DANIEL
In the Outer Hebrides.

CARDINAL
Dead and in the Outer Hebrides?

UNCLE STURTEVANT
There is no one here but us.

DANIEL
And Mr. Godot.

LUCILLE
And the Pope.

CARDINAL
(Alarmed)
Oh. Oh, no.

ALICE
What's the matter?

CARDINAL
Are you sure I'm dead?

ALICE
Yes.

CARDINAL
May I confess?

ALICE
It might make you feel better.

UNCLE STURTEVANT
You may face Purgatory.

DANIEL
Or beyond.

CARDINAL
Beyond?

DANIEL
Heaven is beyond Purgatory.

CARDINAL
We killed the Pope.

EVERYONE
What?!

CARDINAL
There was a cabal against him, and we killed him.
(Everyone is dumbfounded)

LUCILE
What on earth?

CARDINAL
I know, I know. Well, even the new millennium can contain a few old jokes.

DANIEL
Jokes?

CARDINAL
I was to replace him.

DANIEL
As Pope?
(The CARDINAL nods)

DANIEL
Oh.
(SHEPHERD begins to cry)

DANIEL
(Pointing to the SHEPHERD)
What about him?

CARDINAL
He was my catamite.

DANIEL
I thought he was a Shepherd, looking for his sheep.

SHEPHERD
I went astray.

CARDINAL
He just wandered in one day, and I took him.

SHEPHERD
I tried to resist.

CARDINAL
It was only a one-night stand.

SHEPHERD
It hurt.

DANIEL
I am sure it did. Look here.
(To the CARDINAL)
Do you think you might do this boy a penance?

CARDINAL
Anything.

DANIEL
Help him find his sheep.
(SHEPHERD and CARDINAL exit)

LUCILLE
Where's Papa?

UNCLE STURTEVANT
The Pope is exploring the Hinterlands.

ALICE
I saw him a while ago North-Northwest of here.

DANIEL
Shall I go find him?

LUCILLE
Let him find us. There is not much out there, and we are here, and he will come back.

DANIEL
What if he meets the Cardinal?

LUCILLE
Such is the difficulty of death: sooner or later you meet up with every one of the people you don't want to see.

DANIEL
Slaves.

UNCLE STURTEVANT
Victims.

LUCILLE
The ugly.

ALICE
The powerful.

UNCLE STURTEVANT
The crazies we wronged.

LUCILLE
The crazies we were.

DANIEL
We have already examined ourselves.

LUCILLE
And our histories.

UNCLE STURTEVANT
Our past.

LUCILLE
Now we are better.

UNCLE STURTEVANT
Now we are better off.

LUCILLE
I suppose.

DANIEL
What about the Pope and the Cardinal?

LUCILLE
Sooner or later we'll get them together –

DANIEL
And see what happens.

LUCILLE
Yes.

UNCLE STURTEVANT
Yes.

ALICE
Yes.

DANIEL
Yes.

ACT II

SCENE 4

Another part of the Outer Hebrides.
>POPE

This looks familiar.
(The POPE gazes into the audience. Then he turns to upstage right and left)
>POPE

Where am I?
(SHEPHERD appears)
>SHEPHERD

Sir?
>POPE

Child?
>SHEPHERD

I am lost.
>POPE

I am, too.
>SHEPHERD

I was abused.

POPE
I was, too. Now we are free, to be ourselves.

SHEPHERD
But I am not grown-up. How can I ever realize myself? How can I grow up, now that I am dead?

POPE
(Crying)
The things we do to satisfy ourselves.

SHEPHERD
Are you my master?

POPE
Master? Here?

SHEPHERD
There is no one else.

POPE
I suppose I can volunteer.

SHEPHERD
I cannot find my master, nor my sheep – except one.

POPE
One?

SHEPHERD
Yes, one. He was dressed all in red.

POPE
Red?

SHEPHERD
Yes.

POPE
Did he have horns?

SHEPHERD
I don't know.

POPE
A tail?

SHEPHERD
Maybe. But I didn't really notice. I don't know. I am only a boy.

POPE
It must have been the Devil. Or the Anti-Christ.

SHEPHERD
Who are they?

POPE
(Ignoring him)
I knew I would have to deal with him sooner or later.

SHEPHERD
Sooner or later?

POPE
Yes.

SHEPHERD
I am afraid.

POPE
Don't be afraid. Please. I'll help you. But you must help me find him. He is very dangerous.

SHEPHERD
I have a rope.
(SHEPHERD produces the rope)

POPE
Good. Let's see if we can track him down.
(They wander off)

ACT III

SCENE 1

The POPE enters with SHEPHERD GIRL.

GIRL
Where did he go?

POPE
Who go?

GIRL
My brother.

POPE
I thought you were he.

GIRL
I am a girl.

POPE
You must be twins.

GIRL
Others have noticed a resemblance.

POPE
What is your name, child?

GIRL
Perdita.

POPE
Oh, dear. I seem to remember that name.
(SHEPHERD BOY enters)

POPE
There you are.

PERDITA
Ulysses!

SHEPHERD
That is not my name.

POPE
(To PERDITA)
Are you sure you have the right one?

PERDITA
No. But I think if the name fits.

SHEPHERD
I am called Candide, Candy for short.

POPE
Now I know why everyone liked you so much.

CANDY
I thought they all hated me.

POPE
Same thing.

PERDITA
You gave them indigestion.

POPE
Worse.

PERDITA
Where are we?

CANDY
We are looking for a red person.

PERDITA
But where are we?

POPE
Someone said this was Purgatory.

PERDITA
What? It can't be. I'm not dead.

CANDY
That's what you think.

POPE
We are looking for a dead Cardinal.

PERDITA
A bird? In the Outer Hebrides? I mean, Purgatory?

POPE
Who told you about the Outer Hebrides?

PERDITA
It just looked familiar.

POPE
Have you been here before?

PERDITA
I come from here, like my brother.

POPE
Oh.

PERDITA
Anyway, I have seen a man dressed in red.

POPE
With horns?

CANDY
And a forked tail?

POPE
He carries a large fork.
(PERDITA looks confused)

CANDY
To spear souls. He eats them. On the run.

PERDITA
We are all on the run.

POPE
It is time to make a stand.

CANDY
Yes. I am tired of running.

PERDITA
Me, too.

POPE
Then we must find the Cardinal that killed me. Avant!
(The CARDINAL appears upstage, then runs off)

PERDITA
Was that him?

POPE
I didn't have my glasses on.

CANDY
He looked familiar.

POPE
They all look the same.

CANDY
Very conservative.

POPE
Backward looking.

PERDITA
I try always to look progressive. That is where the future lies.

POPE
Our future is stretching before us.

CANDY
What about the Cardinal?

POPE
He's not going anywhere.

PERDITA
We are – we are conquering ourselves, and that is a step in the right direction.

CANDY
You mean there is a way out of Purgatory?

POPE
There has to be.
(CANDY starts to cry)

CANDY
I didn't choose to be a catamite.

POPE
I am so sorry.

PERDITA
I didn't choose to die.

CANDY
Don't tell us. It will give me the horrors.

PERDITA
You already have the horrors.
(The POPE, CANDY, and PERDITA are all silent)

CANDY
I am afraid.

POPE
I feel a bit peppy.

PERDITA
A bright future can change your day.

POPE
How old are you?

CANDY
She's fourteen.

POPE
(To CANDY)
And you?

PERDITA
Nineteen.

POPE
Then you can't be twins.

PERDITA
Then we are an optical illusion.

POPE
Maybe I am hallucinating.

CANDY
I don't think so.
(The POPE looks dazed)

PERDITA
You are a former Pope. No wonder you are confused.

POPE
I am your superior, and I am not confused.

PERDITA
Yes, you are. You think you aren't, but you are. Very confused.

POPE
I have never in my life been confused.

PERDITA
You are not alive, and you have always been confused. Now that you are dead, *(indicating herself and Candy)* we are going to reform you. That is why we are here. Then all three of us can get out of Purgatory.

(The POPE is silent)

POPE
Where do you propose to begin?

PERDITA
With the Cardinal.

CANDY
And my sheep.

POPE
Sheep, sheep, can you think of anything else?

CANDY
It is better than thinking of you.

PERDITA
Stop! Be constructive. Mr. Pope, you are dead and, therefore, superior to no one. It is just like being mad in a madhouse. There are no social grades here. We are not a cast society.

POPE
But this is an exclusive neighborhood!

CANDY
Think again.

POPE
You mean I have to listen to the wisdom of a fourteen-year-old girl?

CANDY
(To POPE)
What do you know? What brought you here? Your experience can't be too deep, nor your knowledge.

POPE
Death is deep.

PERDITA
Death is what you make of it, just like life. It looks to me like you have failed in both.
(The POPE is astounded)

POPE
Now look here, if you are going to lecture me, I will sic that Cardinal on you.

PERDITA
Nonsense. He's just like you, only worse. I am not afraid of either of you. All you can do now is mock me, and mocking is an empty weapon.

POPE
Dear Lord, preserve me from young girls.

CANDY
I thought He had. Where is He anyway?
(GODOT enters with full cast except CARDINAL)

GODOT
Do I have a voice?
(To PERDITA)
And who are you?

PERDITA
A dead duck.

POPE
Duckling.

PERDITA
He just dislikes me because I am a girl and smarter and prettier than him.

GODOT
(To POPE)
Have you been abusing people again?

POPE
People?

GODOT
A poor Shepherd without sheep and his sister.

POPE
They abuse me.

PERDITA
We are trying to educate him to the realities of death, and he is being unrealistic.

POPE
(To PERDITA)
What do you know?

GODOT
(To POPE)
Quiet!
(To PERDITA)
The truth sometimes has to be approached obliquely, as though you were trying to catch a wild cat.

PERDITA
Can we tame him?
(Everyone looks dubious)

GODOT
That is my stock-in-trade.

POPE
Youth is cruel – it has certainly been cruel to me.

PERDITA
Age has its limits.

GODOT
Providence has brought us together. Let us find out why.
(The CARDINAL enters with choker around his neck and chain dragging behind him)

GODOT
Ah! *Le Nouveau Venu.*

CARDINAL
Please don't accuse me of social climbing.

POPE
(With venom.)
You do not do yourself justice.

GODOT
(To POPE)
Wait your turn, please.

POPE
But he killed me, with his own heart. Blackguard! He was a *poseur* and ingratiated himself. I trusted him.
(POPE begins to cry)

CARDINAL
It is your own fault. You are a fool. You take yourself too seriously.

POPE
Beast!

GODOT
A little quiet, please.

CARDINAL
It was a secret decision of the College of Cardinals. His wrongs and insufficiencies were too great to tolerate. It is all your own fault. It was the only way out we could devise.

GODOT
If you two do not stop, I will send you back to life.

POPE
You!?

CARDINAL
You!?

UNCLE STURTEVANT
All we need is a little love.
(Everyone astounded, looks at him)

LADY DALY
(To STURTEVANT)
What are you, a weak reed?

DOTTIE
You look a bit dusty. Would you like to be cleaned?

LUCILLE
How about a stiff gin?

ALICE
I could serve you something. Today's special is tongue with raspberries and orange sauce.

LANCELOT
I could analyze. *Pro bono.*

LADY DALY
Pro bono publico.

DANIEL
I could offer them my innocence.

GODOT
You're too late.

POPE
It's never too late to say goodbye.
(POPE does not move)

GODOT
Your slip is showing.
(POPE searches his raiment. He brings out a rabbit)

POPE
(Perplexed)
Where did that come from?

PERDITA
Dinner.

GODOT
We don't eat here.

POPE
Then why is it here?

CARDINAL
You ought to know.

POPE
I know nothing.

CARDINAL
At last, the truth.

POPE
You have all set me up.

DOTTIE
He doesn't look like a Rabbit.

LADY DALY
Looks aren't everything.

LANCELOT
There are more –

LADY DALY
Where that came from.

(POPE pulls out a frog)

LUCILLE
Haute cuisine.

ALICE
Frog legs.

(POPE pulls out a dinner bell. He rings it)

GODOT
Yes, flesh is perishable.

LADY DALY
And edible.

GODOT
Here, we do not eat.

DOTTIE
They will make nice pets.

(They all look at POPE and CARDINAL)

POPE
I am not a pet.

(CARDINAL takes off choker and chain)

CARDINAL
Me, neither.

LANCELOT
Let us drive them into each other's arms.
(POPE and CARDINAL back away from each other)

DANIEL
The repulsion of the same.

GODOT
We are achieving something.
(POPE and CARDINAL embrace)

DANIEL
The laws of physics have been reversed.

GODOT
No. We are just seeing the final conjugation of evil.

POPE
What?

CARDINAL
What?

DOTTIE
I think they are going to Hades.

GODOT
We call it Hell. They love each other. They created it on earth, now they can enjoy their time together permanently.

POPE
(To GODOT)
You are an imposter.

GODOT
You are the imposter. And your Cardinal is only a pale shadow of yourself.

CARDINAL
We are not afraid of you.

GODOT
We are not afraid of you. Take off those clothes.

CARDINAL
(Embraces POPE)
It is too cold.

GODOT
You will not miss what you haven't earned. Take them off.
(CARDINAL drops cape and miter)

GODOT
(To POPE)
Your turn.
(POPE follows suit)

GODOT
Now you can love each other as it suits you.
(POPE and CARDINAL look at each other, first in disbelief, then with growing aversion)

GODOT
(To DANIEL)
Tie them together. They have created their own permanent bond.

LUCILLE
(To POPE and CARDINAL)
May I offer you a sloe gin?
(POPE and CARDINAL drink glass of gin like water)

LUCILLE
That was quick.
(LUCILLE refills their glasses. They drink again, this time savoring their drinks)

LUCILLE
Take your time.
(LUCILLE refills glasses. She hands Pope her bottle of gin)

LUCILLE
We have more.
(POPE and CARDINAL begin to laugh)

GODOT
What a couple.

DOTTIE
Very sweet.

GODOT
They have found themselves.

DANIEL
They have found each other.

LANCELOT
A light love for a dark pair.

ALICE
I can take care of them.

GODOT
Let them take care of each other. We have to prepare for the next wave. I see a lot of red rising in the distance.

DANIEL
We get the whole College of Cardinals?

GODOT
Rome has exploded.
(Everyone is surprised)

GODOT
Metaphorically, of course. But I do anticipate some more company.

DANIEL
Where are they all going to sleep?

GODOT
With their souls.

DANIEL
Alone?

GODOT
I should think so.

DANIEL
What about the sheep?

CANDY
Now they are free.

DANIEL
You found them?

CANDY
I have let them go for good.

DANIEL
For good?

GODOT
Very good.

CANDY
Now Perdita and I can go home.

PERDITA
We are home.

GODOT
Join us, if you like.

CANDY
Now that my sheep are free, so am I.

PERDITA
And me.

GODOT
You have all been arrested. Now you are free.

DANIEL
What about those two?

LUCILLE
They have found each other.

DANIEL
They can't see.

GODOT
Right.

LUCILLE
Do they have a future?

GODOT
That is still to be seen. Some choices flow in one direction only, like time.

DANIEL
You mean they are tied together for eternity.

GODOT
Unless they choose nothing. That is their only hope.

DOTTIE
Hope?

LADY DALY
I would call that hope forlorn.

GODOT
For them it is the sole way out.

DANIEL
Dear Godot.

LANCELOT
When does the red stampede hit us?

GODOT
They will take their time. First, they must make up their minds what to do.

DANIEL
Do they know how to choose?

GODOT
As well as I or you.

DANIEL
I see fire in your eyes.

GODOT
They will ask me to give you up.

DANIEL
But we love each other.

GODOT
That is why they want me to give you up.

DANIEL
Can't we share our love with everyone?

GODOT
It is possible.

DANIEL
Will they permit it?

GODOT
Look.
(POPE and CARDINAL, tied together, try to walk)
(POPE and CARDINAL manage to hop offstage)

LANCELOT
Imagine that!
(LANCELOT looks in disbelief at the retreating couple)

ACT III

SCENE 2

Scene opens with entire cast seated around DANIEL, CANDY, PERDITA, and GODOT, officiating. PERDITA is dressed as for marriage, and stands between the other two young men.

    GODOT
Are we ready?

    PERDITA
Oh, Mr. Godot, I am frightened.

    CANDY
I am too young to get married.

    DANIEL
I am too old.

    GODOT
First, pretend it is the rehearsal, and everything will be fine. Now, Perdita, do you take Candy and Daniel in the civil bond of love?

    PERDITA
I suppose so.

    GODOT
Please.

PERDITA
Yes.

GODOT
And you, Daniel, and Candy, do you both take Perdita in the civil bond of love?

CANDY
Yes.

DANIEL
Yes.

GODOT
And Candy, do you take Daniel as your love?

CANDY
Yes.

GODOT
And, Daniel, do you take Candy in love?

DANIEL
Isn't he a little young?

CANDY
Nonsense.

GODOT
His experience makes up for his youth. Daniel?

DANIEL
I do.

GODOT
Now all three of you may kiss each other.
(They do)

DANIEL
(To GODOT)
I still love you.

GODOT
That is alright. Just be willing to share me with the rest of the world.

DANIEL
Dead or alive?

GODOT
At this point, the dead outnumber the living; after all, the Universe have been around longer than Earth, and individuals have been passing away for a good part of that time.

DANIEL
Then the Universe is full of other souls?

GODOT
Anywhere you care to go.

UNCLE STURTEVANT
I don't see too many here.

GODOT
Oh no, Uncle. You are a select group.

UNCLE STURTEVANT
When do we join the others?

GODOT
Whenever you wish.

UNCLE STURTEVANT
What?

GODOT
There is a cliff looking out over the sea just a bit south of here. When you are ready, you jump off.

UNCLE STURTEVANT
I cannot fly.

GODOT
You will not. You will not lose yourself, only your body. The rest of you will be translated elsewhere.

UNCLE STURTEVANT
And where is elsewhere?

CAST
Yes?

GODOT
The realm of spirit.

DANIEL
That sounds rather vague.

CANDY
Don't we three get some Honeymoon first?

PERDITA
If we jump off your cliff, we won't be able to consummate our union.

CANDY
Not even in triplicate.

DANIEL
No.

GODOT
You may enjoy each other here for as long as you like.

LADY DALY
They won't last.

(DANIEL, PERDITA, and CANDY look disappointed)

GODOT
I assure you, the further realm of the spirit is far beyond what you can experience here.

LUCILLE
I rather like cocktails.

DOTTIE
Spirits don't collect dust.

LANCELOT
There are no mad people in the beyond.

GODOT
I am afraid your current identities will not extend to the sphere of the beyond.

ALICE
And I thought nobility, even without a title, might be permanent.

GODOT
As I say, you needn't jump until you are ready.

DOTTIE
I don't want to.

GODOT
The present is always becoming the future.

UNCLE STURTEVANT
And vice versa.

GODOT
Yes. And the future is as long as you may wish. When you are tired of Existence, you may get out.

LUCILLE
Opt out?

GODOT
Yes. You may return to Nothing out of which you were born.

DANIEL
What is Nothing?

GODOT

The only truth that can be said about Nothing is that it does not exist.

DANIEL

Then, ultimately, all we face is Nothing.

GODOT

Right.

LADY DALY

Left.

DANIEL

And in between.

UNCLE STURTEVANT

Then why are we here?

GODOT

Anyone?

(All silent)

GODOT

To pass the time. As you wish. Time is the secret of choice, and choice is what you do as long as you enjoy life or death, one form of existence or another.

LANCELOT

Then in the end, it is all the same what we do.

GODOT

Not at all. Your existence has its peculiar shape. That shape is what you choose.

UNCLE STURTEVANT

Can't we abstain?

DOTTIE

I don't want to choose.

GODOT
That is your choice.

LUCILLE
Oh, dear. I think I need a drink.

GODOT
That is your choice.

LADY DALY
I ain't jumpin' off no cliff. That's my choice.

GODOT
Suit yourself. Some day you will tire of all this, and that is the day you will become spirit and realize yourself. Until then, you will merely be a shadow floating on the shore of the Outer Hebrides.

(Godot begins to wrap his garments around him. He slowly rises off the ground. Lights settle on him, shadows engulf the others)

GODOT
I must leave you now.

DANIEL
Dear Mr. Godot, where are you going?

GODOT
Everywhere and nowhere. My destiny was sealed at birth. So was yours. Now, I must visit other people in other worlds. The Universe is vast, and almost all of it lies beyond your comprehension, and even your imagination.

DOTTIE
Oh, Mr. Godot, don't go.

LADY DALY AND OTHERS
Don't leave us. What will happen to us without you?
(GODOT is already gone)

- END -

CODA

GODOT
The life of the heart is almost as difficult as the life of the mind.

DANIEL
Moreso. I know. I have a heart.

GODOT
I do, too. For you.

DOTTIE
What about me?

GODOT
For all of you. But I am particularly attached to Daniel.

UNCLE STURTEVANT
I thought you had to be impartial, that you had to treat us all equally.

GODOT
My mistake.

LADY DALY
It was no mistake. Anyone my color knows that.

GODOT
I am doomed.

DANIEL
Not at all. You have our love, love from all of us.

GODOT
Great.

LUCILLE
Are you going to belittle us?
(GODOT assumes tired air)
GODOT
My problems are immense – and universal. Love, love, everywhere you look you fall into a trap. I have gotten tired of the whole set-up. I arranged the possibilities. It was your choice what to do.

LADY DALY
We have heard this before.

UNCLE STURTEVANT
It gets us nowhere.

GODOT
On the contrary, it assures your future.

DANIEL
If we are dead, we don't have a future.

GODOT
If you are dead, that is all you have.

LUCILLE
What about our past?

GODOT
You possess that, too.

DANIEL
So we have memory and anticipation.

GODOT
You can always opt out.

DANIEL
How?

GODOT
Follow the Pope and confine yourself to the eternal present.

ALICE
This is too much for me. I am only a waitress.

GODOT
I am only Godot.

DANIEL
Don't be such a pushover.

UNCLE STURTEVANT
Someone has to tell us what to do!
(Dottie breaks into tears)

GODOT
Let me think. What if I say that you have entered the Great School of Trial and Error?

UNCLE STURTEVANT
You try, we err.

GODOT
I, too, am allowed to err.

DANIEL
How do you know when you are in error?

GODOT
I watch your faces. I listen to your heart. I feel your breath upon my lips and sometimes, late at night, when the whole world is asleep, I cry tears down. That is when I know we are all alive. And we are all alone: even here, together in the Outer Hebrides. Life is a simple puzzle, and once it breaks, you must face the future. I am here to help.

DOTTIE
And we help you, as much as we can.

GODOT

Thank you, Dottie. Thank you all. You have given me your love, and I fear I can only love you back.

LUCILLE

Only?

ALICE

Only?

GODOT

Where does my love get you?

LUCILLE

You have given us back our confidence.

ALICE

You have allowed us to assume our new and real identity.

UNCLE STURTEVANT

You have touched us so that we can never forget.

DANIEL

You have taken away our pain.

LADY DALY

You have made me strong.

LANCELOT

You have weakened my false power, so that I can use it in a new shape for new purposes.

LADY DALY

Love is very powerful, Mr. Godot. Even yours has power. And you must not let yourself think that your mission here or anywhere else is inconsequential. You have found us, you have changed what you found, and we will always be in your debt. So we owe you our future, dead or alive, and we are glad of it. What else could we ask for?

DANIEL
Oh, Mr. Godot, you have helped so much!

LUCILLE
Is there a cocktail in the house?

GODOT
Lucille, I will have a stiff gin martini.

DOTTIE
Champagne for the homeless and unoccupied!

ALICE
(Serving champagne)
Now I am occupied.

DANIEL
Let us all be occupied with something.

UNCLE STURTEVANT
Life – and Death – present us with a great opportunity.

LUCILLE
I want to live!

GODOT
So do I. And I think I can do it with you – through you, and you through me!
(All form a circle around Godot and toast him)

GODOT
Now I must leave you again. Do not forget me.

DANIEL
I cannot.

LADY DALY
Nor I.

DOTTIE
Nor I.

GODOT
Dear Dottie, you remind me of myself in my youth.

DANIEL
Oh, Mr. Godot, were you ever young?

GODOT
I am older than those hills, and once I had a history. And before that –

DANIEL
The night was everywhere.

DOTTIE
Now we are somewhere.

ALICE
And each one of us is someone.

GODOT
I hope in my absence you will take care of one another. I have, indeed, set you up. Now you may proceed on your own.
(POPE and CARDINAL enter)

GODOT
You may begin by giving those two a little instruction.
(GODOT rises out of sight)
(Lights shine on POPE and CARDINAL in rags, still chained to each other)
(BLACKOUT)

-*FINIS*-

www.ingramcontent.com/pod-product-compliance
Lightning Source LLC
Chambersburg PA
CBHW030158100526
44592CB00009B/342